Dear D.

I have a feeling that you may relate to some of the poems in this book. This has been the last year and a half for us.

I wish you good health and happiness

In the Bards with

Love, Jane

Also by Jane H. Fitzgerald:
Notes From a Screened-In Porch
Notes From a Secret Garden
Notes From the Bay

NOTES FROM THE
UNDAUNTED

Reviews from Amazon for *Notes From the Bay*

Friendships and love; the passage of time and surviving
A compelling book of verse capturing the fury, serenity and vibrant beauty of the Chesapeake Bay. Organized into five parts which succeed in capturing the expressions of our everyday moods and experiences -- beginnings and endings; friendships and love; the passage of time and surviving. An inspired work!   *~ Carole, January 24, 2017*

Enchanting
Poetry that is easily understood and beautifully written. Makes you feel that you are there and want to put your feet in the sand. I highly recommend it to any poetry lover.   *~ Joan H., March 28, 2017*

NOT TO BE MISSED!
Although I have never had the pleasure of being on or near Chesapeake Bay Jane's poetry transports me there and lets me experience her experiences, moods and inner thoughts. Her poem FRIENDS goes straight to the heart! A real treasure for all to enjoy!
     ~Amazon Customer, February 23, 2017

Delightful
Delightful poetry about the Bay. Loved it. Definitely recommend this book   *~ Lynsie B., March 2, 2017*

Five Stars
Excellent insight.
     ~ hamiam, January 6, 2017

NOTES FROM THE
UNDAUNTED

*Poems about one man's
journey with cancer*

By Jane H Fitzgerald

Photos by: Jane H. Fitzgerald
Design by: Victoria Capewell Leitch

© 2017, Bay Media, Inc.
No part of this book may be
reproduced without permission of
the publisher. Permission will be
granted for educational purposes.

ISBN: 978-0-9823354--4

BAY MEDIA, INC.

550M Ritchie Highway, #271 I Severna Park, MD 21146
410-647-8402 I www.baymed.com

Dedication

*This book is dedicated to my husband
who has persevered
through a difficult journey*

table of contents

preface

The poems in this book explore one man's struggle with cancer.

My husband, Bruce Fitzgerald, was diagnosed with stage four metastasized melanoma in April of 2016. He received treatment at Johns Hopkins Hospital in the Sidney Kimmel Comprehensive Cancer Center. This is his story told in poetic form expressing both of our perspectives.

Anyone who has suffered with cancer, or has had a relative or friend, who has walked this path, will relate to these poems which are both sad and uplifting. This journey has many universal stops on its complicated route. It's very cathartic to realize that others are having similar experiences and emotions.

There are now revolutionary treatments, which are changing cancer from a once deadly diagnosis to one of extending lives with the possibility of a total cure. Hopefully, this book will help patients deal with the travails of traveling the Cancer Road.

We are very grateful to Dr. Evan Lipson for his excellent care and to Sidney Kimmel for his contributions that made The Sidney Kimmel Cancer Center and Cancer Research Center possible.

Jane H. Fitzgerald
Annapolis, Maryland
November 2017

vantage point

He's a solitary silhouette
on a windswept point
Weighted by the crucible
of an illness like a howling tempest
The roiling sea and craggy boulders
are like vivid images of his inner self
Rough paintings of a rugged path
blind fate has thrust upon him
He stands alone unflinching
Braced against the gusting gale
Divining his destiny

Discovery

It was a routine X-ray
No need for concern
The benign black machine
Revealed a deadly secret
Something round
Like a quarter or a button
A foreign object
Defiling my lung
The anomaly cried fear
Could it be cut out
Excised forever
Or would it explode
Before the trained
Bomb squad
Could diffuse it
Was there time
To save my life
The days would declare
Human intervention or fate
Which would prevail

Jane

The clock captured my being
The minutes were like
An infinite horizon
Time creating fearful dread
At the zenith of anxiety
The surgeon appeared
Guiding me to a private room
Dangerous alarms struck my heart
One half of a lung removed
Cancer
I fought to stay in the light
Disbelief flooded my floundering mind
The next week pathology
Proclaimed a more dire fate
Melanoma
Time bestowed hell
Cancer spread to his liver
Waves of panic threatened to drown me
Future visions were daunting
Like a descending curtain forming
A wall of black loneliness
Normal existence suddenly extinct
I struggled with panic attacks
Sleepless nights with horrifying images
Truth was like a prison, inescapable
I sought solace in friends, hymns, prayer
Endeavoring to stay steady
I battled the terrible tide of terror
Carrying us toward purgatory

I determined to survive
Unwavering by his side
Discovering dormant strength
I would navigate the unknown
perilous journey with him
Together
For better or for worse

Jane and Bruce,
1964.

the invader

—⁓∞⁓—

The sun rose glowing once again
The newspapers arrived on time
The comforting smell of coffee
floated through the rooms
All was right with the world
When without warning
a warring Invader
entered our souls and bodies
Unwilling to acknowledge it
we attempted ignorance
Its persistent presence
pounded our minds
No mountain of wishing
could expel this evil stranger
Its strength and malignancy
forced us to struggle
We were exposed
Brutally vulnerable as if
chained at gunpoint or
lost on a shrouded battlefield
Our days transformed into an
unending contest
against a virulent enemy within
Hope was like reaching for a star
Our mornings rose with sorrow
Our evenings faded in fear
Life will never, ever again
Be the simple enjoyment

of just mornings with
the radiant sunrise
coffee
and
newspapers

Doctor

He's young
He could be our son
But we look upon him
As a sacred savior
Our lives are in his power
We anxiously study him
Scrutinizing test results
We are strangely still
Not wanting to disturb
Anticipating a decision
He finally looks up
Does he know that
We can hardly breathe
His every word a glimmer of hope
The results are vague
He's describing possibilities
Encompassing life and death
Nothing certain, the field is new
Time will tell a partial story
Survivors are recent statistics
He shakes our hands
He appears neither sad nor glad
He's a scientist, a researcher
A man with a mission
Seeking a trail blazing cure
We are the problem and the answer
Work with haste doctor
Discover the weapon
That will still the killer inside
Time is our enemy

waiting room

We are waiting, waiting
Moments to months
For the miracle treatment
Why are we hanging on
What invisible force keeps us here
A mysterious life line holds us
No matter how long we linger
We still long to live
Most see death advancing
at a comfortably distant date
In death's grim anteroom
It's hovering overhead
Ready to pounce
To transport all away
To some uncertain sphere
The sick cleave to hope
Enduring endless distress
Bleak windowless rooms
Full of stifling stale air
Totally lifeless color
Willing to trade their souls
For another day of waiting

"...no matter how long we linger
we still long to live..."

positron emission tomography

PET Scan
A test of discomfort to some
torture to others
No food, no drink, entering empty
Fluid flooding every cavity with
racing radioactive tracers
Expert detectives at
unveiling the covert invader
Strapped in a claustrophobic tube
Like a tightly wrapped mummy
in a symbolic sarcophagus
Struggling not to imagine
the mechanical coffin's findings
Physical hunger assails
Emotional cravings overpower all
Fear of the unknown
Prompts blackening panic
PET SCAN verdict
Possible reprieve
Or
Deadly revelation

"...expert detectives at
unveiling the covert invader..."

phlebotomy

It's crowded, rows of patients
sitting uncomfortably close
Church like quiet
Waiting, as if at a wake
Concealed bald heads
Masks blocking identity
Young, old, rich, poor
foreign, black, white
Microcosm of the world
Dozing, texting, reading
Anxiety is like a thick cloud
pressing down
Telltale blood tests
bequeath hidden secrets
A byway to the unknown
What will the red rivers reveal
A liquid prophesy
Auger of the struggle to survive
Blood
Flowing with vibrant health
Blood
Carrier of portending death
Blood

"...A byway to the unknown..."

Treatment Room

The treatment room defies
the bleak waiting room
It's bright and busy
The incessant beeping
of the infusion monitors
mimic myriads of heart beats
that throb with cancer
The machines measure life
Drip by drip
Until the bags are empty
Filling the patients with hope
The nurses rush about
Their overly forced joviality
Compensating for the truth
Crowded chairs and beds
offer window views
A distraction from the drip,
the next step, fear
The Treatment Room is a scene
of struggle
To hold on and to let go
It's a stop, a bump
On the path of life
Or a deep chasm
On the road to death

"It's a stop, a bump
on the path of life,..."

Immunotherapy

I'm sitting with virulent chemicals
Dripping steadily into my arm
Coursing through my veins
Like pollutants flowing to the sea
An experimental treatment
Promising, results unknown
Still, I'll grab the chance
It beats eminent death
I'll gamble with Russian Roulette
A Hail Mary Pass
Other patients receive infusions
Suffering through chemotherapy
They will slowly lose their hair
Like leaves drifting in the fall
Destination winter, or if lucky, spring
They will feel nauseous, lose weight
Become walking symbols of disease
Immunotherapy is more insidious
No predictable outward signs so far
A month, a year or more after treatment
A serious, or fatal reaction could strike
It's like a gun pointed at my head
Maybe the next chamber will be empty
And the next? How many chances?
My body is part of a study
Will my torture benefit the future?
My life prolonged as a bullseye
Anticipating the perfect shot
Thankful and Terrified
For my Savior and Killer

my children

My children know I'm mortal
Intellectually, not emotionally
I've always been there
An anchor, a safety line
Predictable, loving, giving
Annoying with my routines
My idiosyncrasies
Expectations and criticisms
I'm their father, loving beyond
Each time they say goodbye
Wondering, will it be the last?
They try to be supportive
Sitting all day in the hospital
Offering help
Can they imagine life without me?
There will be a deep void
They will grieve, tears will flow
In a short time, an unsettling
Realization will possess them
My life stood between them
And their own mortality
An unwanted vision
Will manifest itself
Looking back at them
In the mirror
The older generation

The Director

A plaque on her desk reads
"Director of First Impressions"
The absurdity of it is laughable
Its profoundness immeasurable
The bewildered patients
Lined up in chairs on precipices
Inching toward the fall
Souls wandering through thick trees
Dripping with anxiety
Treading paths of fearful mazes
Shrouded in clouded awareness
Catching clues for cures
From dangerous dark laboratories
Producing illusive studies
Promising possible light
A covenant of belief and science
Twirling through time
The" Director of First Impressions"
Is like a smiling manikin
Brightly displayed, selling hope
Gift wrapping the truth
Losing blood with each stony smile
Until at last
There are no more Impressions

faithful friends

Friends were shocked still
Like sailboats suddenly in the doldrums
The news flew as fast
As gulls plunging for fish
Stage four metastasized melanoma
The words were like mammoth waves
Violently crashing upon all
Drowning out the present
The future taken on the tides
People looked at him differently
Their eyes slightly averted
Hesitant to ask about his health
The stalwarts never stopped calling
Treating him with medicinal hope
Feeling their concern and camaraderie
He confided in them
They offered a stress releasing lifeline
He would have drowned alone
Their loving kindness saved his morale
Rescuing him from the devastating broadside

Endless Waiting

Each minute is an agonizing
crucible
Anticipating cancer test destiny
Longing for unveiled truth
Emotions raw like a prisoner's
on death row
Waiting, waiting
Endless nightmare of uncertainty
Technicians and radiologists
Please have mercy
Unchain my heavy heart
Work with jet like speed
Deliver my destiny
Life and death words printed
on winged paper
Flying me to heaven or hell
Whatever it may be
Nothing is more torturous
Than cruel dark ignorance
Will there be another sunrise
or is it
The final death of days

"...waiting, waiting endless
nightmare of uncertainty..."

surgical mask

Will this small piece of gauze
Keep me safe
A thin window blocking a force
More powerful than life
It is masked hope
Maybe the deadly germs
Will flee in fear
I look so strange
This is my protection
A barrier on my face
Hiding the truth
A delusory veil
My David against Goliath

...my david
against goliath...

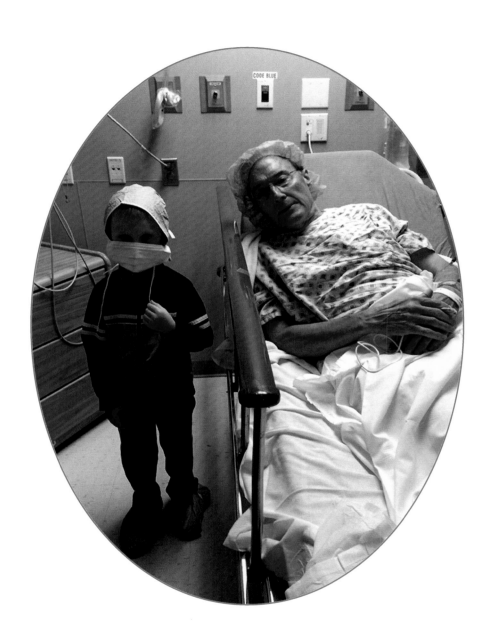

22 Jane H. Fitzgerald

watching

I'm watching him now
Very carefully
For the slightest sign
Of a reaction to a drug
That will either
Save or kill him
I'm like a hunter in a blind
Aware of the slightest movement
On guard, ready to react
Don't move, don't panic
Remember the phone number
A quick response could make
All the difference
Stay alert
My body so tense
Finger gripping the trigger
Rest, will it ever come
No, not now, not after,
Never

"...for the slightest sign of a
reaction to a drug that will
either save or kill him..."

caller id unknown

— ❧ —

Instinct instructed, don't answer
My hand acted like a mindless appendage
The Unknown Caller, my doctor,
Rang at 9 am on a holiday weekend
The familiar voice froze my heart
The timing was like sunbeams at midnight
Morning portending darkness
Go to the hospital ER Immediately
Blood test results mania
Delving into my mysterious body
The code unbreakable
An indefinite answer
Take two pills, return in two days.
Another blood draw prophesy
Let thoughts of mortality
Fall flashing away
Like comets from the sky
Forget yourself in books, booze,
drugs, food, fantasy, whatever
For the possibility may be that
You are
Lost forever

"...The timing was like
sunbeams at midnight..."

the ER

It's the morning before Christmas
We are frantically racing to the ER
A white coat settles us in a tiny cubicle
adjacent to a criminal in shackles
guarded by two laconic policeman
In haste we had abandoned
a colorful holiday table
Never to be graced by guests
It could be any day in the ER
For us it was to have been
a celebration of togetherness
Instead it's tubes and beeps
Waiting, endless waiting
Can they bring us back from the edge
Did we notify all the guests
Did we turn the oven off
The chained man is escorted
by an armed blue suit
for a bathroom break
We are held tightly captive by
one plastic bag after another
Dripping drops of hope toward
another phantom holiday
Fate suspended from a pole
Results slowly emerging
The agony of not knowing
Did we lock the front door
Is the dog in her crate
Will the IV revive or drown us

Did we turn the TV off
What will the guests do
Their planned day is empty
Ours is full of excruciating anxiety
Emanating like static from a radio
Pulsating in the cubicle
Flooding the sterile shiny halls
The grim man is unshackled
Discharge papers in hand
We are finally let go, released
But not to freedom
The test results command
Return in two days
The ER is waiting

"...it's the morning
before christmas..."

Name calling

— ❧ —

The list flows endlessly
like noisy migrating geese
disappearing in the distance
One by one
Names resound, filling the room
Mr. Randall
Mrs. Brown
Mrs. Schwartz
Mr. Leo
Mr. Donovan
Strong healthy voices
call out loudly
Announcing the sickly over
the low din of conversations
silent iPad users
absorbed magazine readers
and unconscious dozers
All waiting for the doctors
Some full of hope
Those too with despair
Patience required for a cure
Tedious hours, months of moons
Perhaps enduring years
If they are lucky or blessed
The summons will be met here
Not by sudden or lingering death
Causing the silent names
to appear in print on
a muted obituary list

Recovery Room Curtains

The sounds of curtains sliding
Echo from
Cubicle after cubicle
Opening and closing
Time after time
Mysterious equipment
Telling tales of
Life and death
Beeping, ringing,
loudly, softly
Clicking wheels of the sick
Chairs, tanks, beds
Doctors, nurses, aides
Anonymous in scrubs
Assailed by noises
Suffering alarm fatigue
Captured by computers
Analyzing test results while
The curtains keep moving
Open and shut
Open and shut

cancer roller coaster

Some days I'm full of expectations
Maybe there is life ahead
I'll be at that graduation
See my grandchild marry
Enjoy another voyage
Feeling anxiety slip away
I'm on the way up
Flying into heady realms
Where sickness is left behind
I'm dizzy with healthy happiness
The plunge strikes without warning
Slamming my breath away
My heart flips frantically
Raging primal screams are lost
In the horrendous horror
of lightening fast free fall
Racing wildly into darkness
A blind black tunnel with no end
I surrender, resigned to death
Anticipating the crushing crash
A slight light appears
Tearing at my trembling heart
Up, up, up
Soaring into brilliant blinding sunlight
Pulling me into the circle of life
Bestowing hope once again
How many times can
I sustain such a horrifying ride
Each time I'm a little weaker

The will to survive lessens
with every blindsiding
twist and turn
The roller coaster is a cruel torture
Will I get off alive
Is there solid ground in sight
I'm caught in a ghastly cycle of
hope and despair
Anxiously fearing my destiny

Test After Test

—⁓—

Here I go again
An important definitive test
Revealing the enigma within
Will the cancer be vanished
or is it racing wildly within me
My young doctor prescribes my fate
A promising revolutionary treatment
delivering possible deadly side effects
or maybe many years to come
Life back on the window ledge
An edge with no clear view
Teetering on the brink, losing ground
Afraid of the plunge, of free fall
No nets, no life ring
Maybe God is waiting to catch me
Hold me, escort me into death
It's doubtful God will be there
My path has been too twisted
Too far away from God's waiting room
My destiny is as mysterious
as the black holes in the universe
The unknown is infinite

"... Here I go again..."

waiting Room Revisited

Patients start and end
in the waiting room
Weary eyes portray years of
struggling against painful disease
Faces conceal myriads
of sad secrets
Screaming silently at
life's grim and painful play
Sounds are muted
as though underwater
Pushed down and down
Unable to release the life force
iPhones rule the Waiting Room
offering filtered connection
Eyes looking downward
Blankly turning up
to view the
Wasted
Sitting tightly in rows
against drab windowless walls
like the barren earth
That will offer cold shelter
The permanent, "Resting Place"

"...faces conceal myriads
of sad secrets
screaming silently..."

cautiously optimistic Doctor

Besieged by a deadly disease
Our future is in your hands
Following an experimental path
for a revolutionary cure
Dispatching the demons
with stunning success
Until suddenly splintered
like an ax splitting wood
Concealed side effects
Propelled us in panic
feeling like frightened children
racing to the emergency room
Where your expertise
ordered step by step procedures
Rescuing us from the abyss
Dropping our despair into darkness
Now your judgment and skill
grant us another course
We are like a ship
navigating the rough waters
hopefully finding home
We can almost perceive
Your brain endeavoring
to maneuver the labyrinth
Finding the effective therapy
Your kind interest and intelligence
May bestow upon us
a second chance
to be

free from disease and fear
We all remain steadfastly
Cautiously Optimistic

Dedicated with Thankfulness to Dr. Evan J. Lipson

"...your kind interest and
intelligence
may bestow upon us
a second chance
to be..."

who has cancer?

Walking the hospital halls
are some who are
Twisted, bent, shrunken
spectral images
Others reflect spirit
Begging the question
What thrives inside
Who is the sick one
The wearer of the mask
The wheelchair bound
The heavy set reader
The true level of being
is often camouflaged
like birds hidden in tress
Many are desperate
Enduring endless fear
Asking why
Challenging fairness
Who is facing death
Who is aiding the sick
Unperceived fates sitting
side by side

sick of it

I'm so sick of it all
The endless waiting
Tests, vitals, drips
The sterile hospital
With its shiny floors
Long hallow hallways
Incessant beeping
Declaring danger
Frightening visions
of the walking wounded
Waiting, waiting
I'm so sick, sick of it all
I want to feel normal again
Happy and hopeful
Looking forward to life
Not death
I'm on this path with
Thoughts and feelings
Greater in scope
Than any hospital
The road is shorter
Day by day
My years have added up
It's a final drawn out stage
That forces me inward
Closer to death
Touching more intensely
By unrelenting cancer

constant companion

He appeared unchanged
He acted fine
No one would know
What hid inside
The deadly demon lurked
A constant companion
When dynamically engaged
The menacing specter receded
In the dark stillness of night
It crushed him in its crippling grip
vanquishing reason and hope
Its constancy tenacious
Denial no longer an option
Fear reigned as victor
Robber of peace
Thief of joy
For the rest of time
Feeling well or sick
The phantom would prevail
Sometimes all powerful
or faintly felt
But always whispering
Concealed in the shadows
Threatening existence
His constant companion

Last Treatment Prophecy

Our emotions are raw
Kept tightly wrapped
We talk of friends, the weather
Never, what if…………
Waiting this time
is like watching for a birth
full of anxiety and expectation
Our patience so thin
We are afraid of drowning
standing on thin ice
Eons later we are summoned
Our name jolts us
Echoing off the walls
We tensely grab
the life line
Guardedly entering the office
The doctor greets us warmly
I'm choking on a primal scream
What's churning unseen
A spread of evil or release
The suspense is deafening
With a caring tone
The doctor carefully explains
cancer is currently banished
Its persistent force
may visit again
But for now it's erased
Tears of relief flood my soul
I'm flying wild like a caged bird

escaping skyward
Carrying the weary weight
up and away
Leaving us lighter, freer
The black path faintly visible
Cancer no longer our identity
It's like a rebirth
We are beyond grateful
for our intelligent, kind doctor
Gifted recipients
of a modern medical miracle
Awake again
Out of the shadows
Washed with sunlight
Filled with precious life

Thank you, Dr. Evan Lipson, July 2017

wherewithal

The dictionary says it is the skill
Needed to get or do something
Wherewithal has taken me
Through many ups and downs
Especially the trips to hell and back
No floundering, staying straight
Others depending on me
Reliable is my name
What will carry me on
Family, friends, pets, reading
It's late, maybe the wherewithal is
Losing strength, abandoning me
Leaving me vulnerable on the
Road to death
Or perhaps never weakening
Steady until my last breath

"...wherewithal has taken me
through many ups and downs
especially the trips to hell and
back..."

cancer reprieve

Reprieve
Is that what we have?
A desperately needed break
from the ax hanging over our heads
Its razor sharp blade eager to kill
Cancer is insidious and cruel
It lurks in the dark alleyways
Waiting, just waiting
to suddenly crush a victim
The doctor's words, cancer free
are a mockery
truth wrapped in false sunshine
Cancer is patient, virulent
Bestowing a brief sense of hope
to its hapless carriers
We will grab the phrase Cancer free
and embrace our chances
Engaging in colorful life once again
The only victory is to live today
The enemy senses a wind change
Great advances in research
are starting to erode its power
There will come a time
when the words, Cancer free
will be obsolete
The scourge will be nonexistent
Until then, we will joyfully accept
Our reprieve

He wasn't the type to worry
Always pragmatic
Pushing aside situations
He couldn't control
The diagnoses hit hard
Very unexpectedly
He'd always been healthy
Stage four melanoma
Half a lung removed
Life changing
He remained positive
Keeping his routines
Not dwelling on the devil inside
A pet scan found Cancer
Had spread to his liver
Fear eroded his edges
But not his core
He carried on
Never complaining or
Asking, why me
The immunotherapy weakened him
Naps and early bedtime
Became commonplace
He endured test after test
Sure that the outcome
Would be positive
He was literally possessed
By a demon
But

He never totally surrendered
To the worst enemy of all
Fear

on Leaving

I'm seventy eight years old
Not a bad run
Always healthy until now
I didn't agonize over choices
Once a decision was made
I never looked back
Not introspective or sensitive
Leading a practical life
Loving my work
The challenges, people, structure
Enjoying my family
Connected to children and dogs
More natural, unfiltered
I like to lead, in ways a loner
My wife has enriched my life
Always up to something
New places, different faces,
Pulling me into technology
Bringing color, movement
Not sure about God or heaven
If this is it, so be it
I've had a good run

"...if this is it,
so be it..."

survival

— ❦ —

Time is impartial
It just happens
Events are random
They strike without warning
It's our reactions
That determine the day
Can we handle the
Success or disappointment
Are we the oak or the willow
An organism is only as healthy
as its ability to change
to endure, persevere
That's survival
That's what we face
Moment by moment
With or without
Consciousness
Until the earth
Marks its claim

"..are we the oak
or the willow..."

the philanthropist

His feet were wet and cold
The cardboard soles
were soaked through
Lunch had been a ketchup sandwich
as unappetizing as moldy bread
It was at that low moment in the rain
that he determined to make money
The Depression had hit his father hard
no work, no income, no pride
He would liberate his family from emptiness
He began by setting up bowling pins
each one a symbol for a dollar
A step toward another life
Drive and perseverance possessed him
A single vision pushed and pulled
By the time he was a teenager
he was supporting his family
A rock for the rest of their lives
Street smarts, luck, hard work
Got him to places far beyond
the reach of a college education
He fought for one deal after another
Working long days and nights
Discovering that he had
an eye for women's clothing
that rivaled prominent designers
Success didn't come like a sudden jackpot

For years he earned significant money and recognition
The Megahit struck when he was about sixty
The world turned and he landed on top
Riches beyond childish dreams were his
A memory of his father guided his next steps
At the height of their poverty
his father had given away half of a windfall
to a friend whose family was starving
That gesture lay hidden in his mind
Now his good fortune would help others
A close friend's daughter
endured an excruciating death from cancer
This deeply emotional experience
pointed him in a direction
Cancer became his crusade
Money took on a new meaning
It wasn't just new shoes
It gave him the power
to make a significant difference
If enough resources were focused on
one of man's greatest enemies
cancer could be defeated
His generosity created state of the art
cancer research hospitals
Thousands of lives would become
beneficiaries of his hard won fortune
His father's losses would be vindicated

He only wished he was still alive to witness
the enriched legacy he had bequeathed
An ever grateful and loving son
whose efforts bestowed
burning rays of hope
to cancer victims
throughout the world

Dedicated with thankfulness to Sidney Kimmel

Poratrait of Sidney Kimmel from the Sidney Kimmel
Comprehensive Cancer Reasearch Center at
Johns Hopkins Hospital Center, Baltimore, Maryland

Epilogue

After fifteen months and two rounds of different types of immunotherapy my husband's cancer is in remission.

Cancer research is constantly breaking barriers and discovering new methods of treatment. There is promising hope for cancer patients, and the possibility that cancer will be eradicated in the coming years.

We are so very thankful to the dedicated professionals at Johns Hopkins Hospital who are at the forefront of this battle. They continue to save lives with their hard work, expertise and extensive research.

Jane and Bruce
August 2017

Legacy

Papa holds my hand
I am so small
He leans down to reach me
Never walking too fast
It doesn't matter where we go
Beach, fishing, ice cream
Papa leads us both
Feeling safe
Always holding hands

cherished

I've joyfully watched them flourish
Celebrating the many milestones
Attempting that first breathtaking step
Crawling speedily like hungry crabs
Holding their tiny toddler hands
Guiding their rods as they gleefully fished
Playing catch on the beach at dusk
Fearfully watching the initial wobbly bicycle
Reliving the familiar through fresh eyes
Rejoicing in them, but sorrowful
Though grown, they are still young
May I be granted more time
To share their expanding horizons
My years have passed
Hopefully they will keep
Hearts warm with love
For a father who
Cherished them so

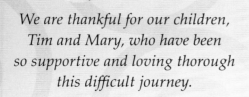

We are thankful for our children,
Tim and Mary, who have been
so supportive and loving thorough
this difficult journey.